fashion DESIGN LOOKBOOK

Walter Foster

© Fleurus Editions - 2014
Published by Walter Foster Publishing,
a division of Quarto Publishing Group USA Inc.
All rights reserved. Walter Foster is a registered trademark.

Publisher: Rebecca J. Razo
Creative Director: Shelley Baugh
Project Editor: Jennifer Gaudet
Senior Editor: Stephanie Meissner
Managing Editor: Karen Julian
Assistant Editor: Janessa Osle
Production Designers: Debbie Aiken, Amanda Tannen
Production Manager: Nicole Szawlowski
Production Coordinator: Lawrence Marquez
English translation by Annette Robichaud

www.walterfoster.com
3 Wrigley, Suite A
Irvine, CA 92618

Printed in China
1 3 5 7 9 10 8 6 4 2
18849

fashion DESIGN

L O O K B O O K

MORE THAN **50** CREATIVE TIPS
AND TECHNIQUES FOR THE
FASHION-FORWARD ARTIST

By Blandine Lelarge

TABLE OF CONTENTS

TOOLS & TIPS

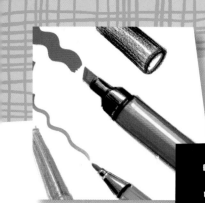

MATERIALS & TOOLS

Each drawing tool has its own set of quirks and limitations, which makes it more or less suited to a particular style. Try a few to see what works for you, and choose the one that best fits your project. Practice and train yourself in each technique, but feel free to mix them up!

Graphite Pencils

Graphite drawing pencils are designated by hardness and softness. H pencils are hard and make lighter marks; B pencils are soft and make darker marks. Pencils range from very soft (9B) to very hard (9H). For fashion drawing, I prefer to use a 2B pencil, which will give your overall design more character.

Tip

FOR THE PROJECTS IN THIS BOOK, I WORK WITH AN ASSORTMENT OF TOOLS AND MATERIALS, FROM ACRYLIC TO WATERCOLOR TO GOUACHE. KEEP IN MIND, HOWEVER, THAT ALL OF THESE PROJECTS CAN BE CREATED USING ANY MEDIUM—EVEN COLORED PENCILS AND MARKERS— SO FEEL FREE TO USE THE TOOLS AND MATERIALS YOU ARE MOST COMFORTABLE WITH.

Drawing Paper

Drawing paper comes in many sizes and is great for working out your ideas and preliminary sketches using graphite or colored pencils. For finished pieces done with markers or felt-tip pens, it is better to use specialty marker paper to avoid bleeding and smudging. Watercolor paper is a textured paper that works best when using acrylic or watercolor paints, as well as gouache and ink.

Colored Pencils & Felt-tip Markers

Felt-tip markers provide a smoother appearance to your drawing, whereas colored pencils offer interesting textural effects: grainy, fuzzy, etc. Both tools are simple and easy to handle, making them great choices for any project, from planning sketches to adding final color.

MATERIALS & TOOLS

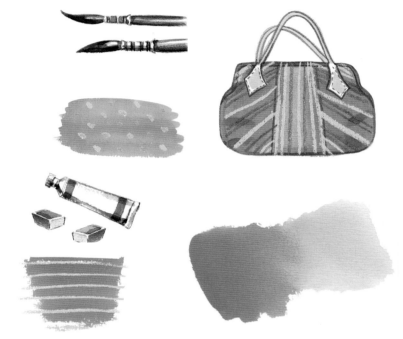

Paintbrushes

Paintbrushes come in a variety of shapes and sizes and are useful for applying all types of paints, from acrylic to watercolor to gouache. Specific shapes and brush types are best for different purposes, such as a round brush with soft hairs for watercolor or a flat brush for creating straight edges and strokes of uniform width. For the projects in this book, you'll need a large (No. 6) brush for applying large swatches of color and a small (No. 4) brush for fine detail work.

Watercolor

Watercolor is prized for its airy and transparent qualities, and it is a popular choice for many fashion designers. It requires a bit of practice to master, but with time you will soon discover how to create form and color with just a few brushstrokes. Watercolor is available in tubes, pans, semi-moist pots, and pencils.

Wax Pastel

Highlight patterns and textures by drawing with wax pastels before applying watercolor paint. The wax repels water and allows the color and texture of the pastel to show through. Always practice your technique on practice paper first; you want to perfect the method before beginning your final drawing.

Acrylic

Acrylic is a fast-drying paint that, when used in layers, creates vivid and dynamic color within any drawing. Apply several layers of the same color to accentuate a satin effect, and use a transparent glaze to create a shiny effect. From tanned skin to patterned clothing, the color combinations that can be created with acrylic paints are endless.

Ink

This technique creates a type of character design that differs in style and mood from other methods. When working with ink, use watercolor paper with an adhesive paper backing to protect and preserve your work. Multiple practice rounds are a must, as the use of ink requires precision and skill, especially when drawing fashion!

Gouache

Gouache is similar to watercolor but thicker in consistency. It forms beautiful, velvety color with very few layers. Start by applying the lighter colors of your drawing; then add the darker colors. Working with gouache and watercolor together creates a vivid drawing with delicate effects.

WORKING WITH GOUACHE AND WATERCOLOR TOGETHER CREATES A VIVID DRAWING WITH DELICATE EFFECTS.

RESEARCH & PLANNING

Before beginning the creative process, fashion designers need to do some research. These basic concepts and terms are easy to learn and will offer you greater freedom as an artist once you master them. How can you imagine a nice dress or pair of pants if the figure doesn't look right? You must sculpt the body before planning the clothing.

Sketches

An essential part of fashion design, sketches allow for as many versions as necessary before beginning the final drawing. The principle is the same for all sketches: Practice over and over until you find the right posture, dress, and appearance. Be patient—all great designers go through this too!

▶ First, the *break*; it sets the tone and personality of the model.

The same model can be *crunched* into different postures.

◀ Mastering *proportions* requires a lot of practice. They must be accurate, as the model should feel comfortable in her clothes!

▶ *Holding*, the centerpiece of fashion design, requires several trials, if only for the fun of creating a variety of unique clothing options and accessories that only you can dream up.

◀ It never hurts to create an *environment* around your model; it may be a storefront, a ballroom, or a runway!

▼ Research and brainstorm *color harmonies* that coordinate with the appropriate technique for the model and style of your choice.

RESEARCH & PLANNING

Correct proportions are based on the average size of a mannequin (5'9" to 5'11") perched on heels. The height of the head determines the proportions of the other parts of the body, which altogether represent a little more than eight times the height of the head.

The drawing method is the same for men and women, except that the build should be slightly wider for men. It's important to stick to simple shapes when you start drawing. The process may seem tedious, but it will help with the proportions of your model.

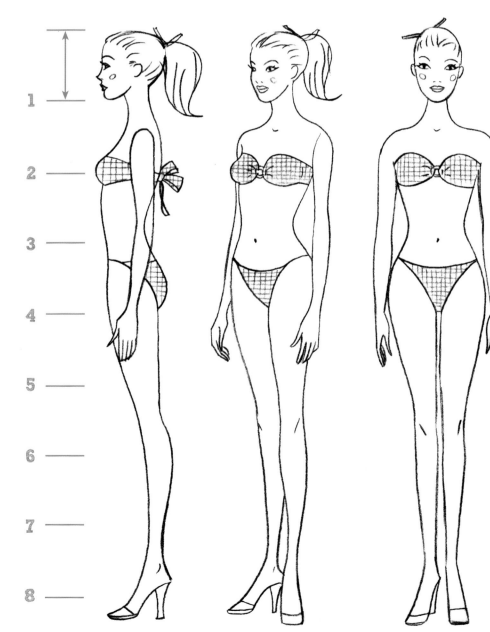

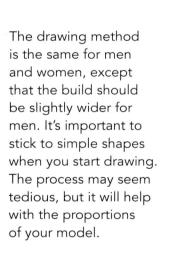

Expressions

Whether sad, happy, or suspicious, your model's expression influences the general effect of the outfit. The expression is mainly defined by facial features: frowning for angry; open smile for happy; eyes wide open for surprised.

COLOR INFLUENCES THE EXPRESSION. FOR EXAMPLE, A BLUISH TINT WILL ENHANCE THE FEELING OF SADNESS COMING FROM THE CHARACTER.

Suspicious

Sad

Happy

Surprised

Peaceful

Serious

Rebellious

HAIRSTYLES

The hairstyle reveals a lot about a girl's personality and sense of style. It completes an outfit just as much as accessories and offers a huge range of possibilities.

THIS 1920s STYLE IS TIMELESS!

SPIKED HAIR CREATES A FUNKY STYLE.

A BUN WITH A SIDE FRINGE AND A SMALL, DROOPING STRAND CREATES A CONFIDENT LOOK.

LONG AND VOLUMINOUS HAIR CREATES A MYSTERIOUS AND BEWITCHING EFFECT.

ACCESSORIES

Our clothes are incomplete without accessories! A simple pendant or nice handbag can make the perfect accent to a small top. Accessories are inseparable from fashion—they either enhance or completely ruin an outfit!

Hats

Hats have been used in fashion for decades, in a variety of styles. A good hat can highlight an outfit, warm our ears, or cover a bad haircut. The hat is a faithful companion to your personal sense of style!

SOME HATS ARE JUST FOR VERY SPECIAL OCCASIONS!

NOTHING LIKE A HAT TO COMPLETE A SOPHISTICATED CUT— OR EVEN COVER UP A RIDICULOUS HAIRSTYLE.

18

Glasses

In recent years, eyeglasses have become a favorite accessory of fashion addicts. Choose from countless styles to pair with an endless number of outfits: practical, studious working-girl eyeglasses; movie star-like shaded sunglasses; or funky and colorful sunglasses for fun, trendy outings.

NECKLACES, EARRINGS, BRACELETS, AND RINGS ARE A FEW OF THE MANY WAYS TO ACCESSORIZE A MODEL'S OUTFIT AND MAKE IT SHINE BRIGHTLY.

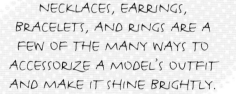

REMEMBER THAT COLOR-MATCHING RULES APPLY!

Jewelry

Jewelry is an essential part of a woman's outfit. As an accessory, jewelry can add to the motif of an outfit. For instance, would you wear diamonds with jeans or costume jewelry with an evening dress?

ACCESSORIES

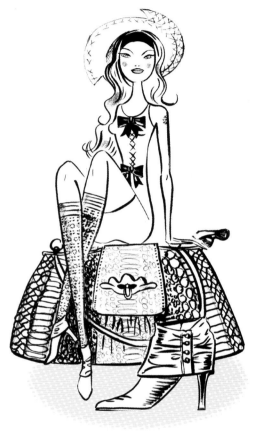

Fashion addict or not, it is impossible to get dressed without shoes—but this necessary staple should not be dismissed as purely functional, as they are also key accessories that reflect trends!

Shoes have allowed women to both express their femininity (heels, boots) and prove their ability to stay on par with men (flat shoes, sneakers). With options ranging from ultra-feminine to tomboy, the possibilities are endless!

Bags

The handbag is a true symbol of lifestyle and personality. Whether a large shopping bag, small handbag, or simple clutch purse, there is a bag for every style!

GOLD ACCENTS, SUCH AS A CLASP OR CHAIN, ADD A GLAMOROUS TOUCH FOR A NIGHT OUT.

A SHORT HANDLE ALLOWS YOU TO CARRY THE BAG BY HAND OR ON THE ELBOW (IN THE ELEGANT FRENCH WAY).

THE CLUTCH PURSE DOES NOT HAVE A LOT OF ROOM, BUT IT PAIRS PERFECTLY WITH A FUR OR COCKTAIL DRESS.

DARE TO COLOR! BUT BE CAREFUL TO COORDINATE THE BAG WITH THE OUTFIT.

NOTHING REPLACES THE PURSE FOR WORKDAYS. IT HOLDS EVERYTHING: MAKEUP, CELLPHONE, KEYS, PENS, ETC.

THE HEIGHT OF CHIC: MATCHING ACCESSORIES TO THE BAG.

FABRICS & PRINTS

For a standout outfit, experiment and play with fabrics and prints. Using different types of fabrics shows creativity and cleverness as a designer.

Materials

FOR A SYNTHETIC EFFECT:
ADD SALT ON A WET WATERCOLOR LAYER AND LET DRY. WHEN THE PAINT IS DRY, REMOVE THE SALT WITH A DRY BRUSH.

FOR A TRANSPARENT, MESH EFFECT:
TRACE THE PATTERN OR RUB THE PAPER WITH A WAX PASTEL. THEN COLOR WITH WATERCOLORS.

FOR A FLUFFY EFFECT:
ADD A LITTLE DILUTED PAINT (ACRYLIC OR GOUACHE) TO A BRUSH, AND TAP IT ON THE PAPER.

FOR A RIBBED WOOL EFFECT:
PAINT A LAYER OF ACRYLIC IN A SOLID COLOR (BROWN). WHEN THE PAINT IS DRY, ADD A SECOND COAT (BEIGE) AND IMMEDIATELY SCRAPE WITH A WOODEN CRAFT STICK.

Fabrics

It is essential to understand how folds form in order to style them. Practice by drawing a scarf casually arranged on a table. Try to simplify the ripples of the fabric. Be especially attentive to the material; some fabrics have rounded folds depicted by curves, while others consist of more angular folds, which are better drawn as zigzags. Finally, ensure you have adequate lighting to accurately shade the shadows.

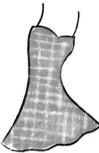

Prints

Prints know no limits—you can mix infinite combinations of colors and patterns!

FOR A SIMPLE LOOK, YOU CAN USE JUST ONE PRINT IN AN OUTFIT.

TO MIX THINGS UP, USE MULTIPLE PRINTS.

OR EVEN TRY MULTIPLE PRINTS ON THE SAME PIECE OF CLOTHING!

THE SAME "RULE" APPLIES FOR ACCESSORIES!

FABRICS & PRINTS

Adding Color

It's easy to create beautifully colored pieces by utilizing warm and cool color schemes. Experiment with various light and dark values to create harmony or contrast for different effects. Start by choosing a range, and then experiment to find the right shades and tones.

WARM AND LIGHT COLOR RANGES:
USE PREDOMINANTLY ORANGE. THE OUTFIT WILL LOOK VERY BRIGHT AND HAPPY.

COLD AND DARK COLOR RANGES:
USE PREDOMINANTLY BLUE. THE OUTFIT WILL LOOK SIMPLE AND SOOTHING.

LIGHT COLORS ADD CONTRAST TO PROCESSED COLD/HOT COLOR RANGES:
THIS SET IS BRIGHT WITHOUT BEING OVERWHELMING.

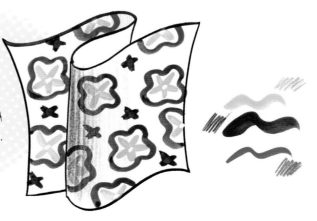

WARM AND DARK COLOR RANGES:
THIS COMBINATION CREATES A RICH IMPRESSION OF FULLNESS.

DIVERSIFY PATTERNS
(JAPANESE-STYLE CHERRY BLOSSOMS,
MINIMALIST SNOWFLAKES, OR
A SET OF COLORED "SCALES"),
WHILE MAINTAINING A SENSE OF
HARMONY AND A GRAPHIC TOUCH.

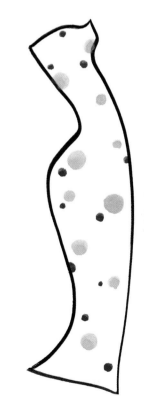

PLAY WITH SPOT SIZES
(ONE SIZE ON THE ENTIRE
DRESS OR A VARIETY OF TWO
OR THREE SIZES) RHYTHMS,
AND COLORS.

STYLED
LOOKS

THE FASHIONISTA

As the name suggests, "fashionistas" are addicts, or victims, of fashion. A true fashionista has expert knowledge of all the latest trends. Nothing escapes her eye! Always in a skirt or dress, she's mastered the art of accessorizing and color-matching to appear perfectly put together for any occasion.

▶ Draw a first draft of the body using simple shapes. Pay attention to proportions!

1

2

◀ Draw in the eyes, nose, and mouth. Sketch the hair with volume and movement. Draw in the scarf, T-shirt, and skirt, as well as the shopping bags and dog. Add detail to the shoes.

3

◀ Finish with small details like prints on the bags, folds in the clothes, and accessories (sunglasses, handbag, makeup, and belt). Don't forget, the dog is also entitled to accessories!

TECHNIQUE: Acrylic

OCHRE
PURPLE
RED
FUCHSIA
MAUVE
BLUE
ORANGE
YELLOW
BLACK

4

▶ Working in layers, allow the paint to dry between each coat. Keep the background plain to bring out the bright colors of the outfit. Respect the harmony of the pink tones—everything must match. Don't use too much water to dilute the paint—the Fashionista likes to be noticed!

HAUTE COUTURE

Materials

- WATERCOLOR PAPER
- HB PENCIL
- ERASER
- BLACK FELT-TIP MARKER
- WAX PASTELS
- WATERCOLOR PENCILS

Fashionistas follow fashion, but the model wearing haute couture inspires it. This fashion-forward girl only wears clothes fresh from the high-fashion runway. Observe haute couture with a careful eye—it will give you an idea of future trends, often a season in advance!

▶ Starting with simple shapes, sketch the outline of the Haute Couture model. Use poses that models usually make on the catwalk.

1

2

◀ Outline some elements of the holding (earrings, shoes), as well as the hair, making it large and sophisticated.

◄ Using a black felt-tip marker, draw each piece of clothing, spending more time adding detail on the printed tunic. Style the hair, and add in the accessories. Don't forget the fishnet leggings!

TECHNIQUE: **Mixed Media**
(Wax Pastel & Watercolor)

ORANGE

MAGENTA

PURPLE

YELLOW OCHRE

GREEN

RED

▶ The Haute Couture model may be a celebrity on the runway, but the real star is her outfit. Apply layers of color in coats; then color the shoes, and add a little touch of makeup. Practice fabric patterns on a loose sheet of paper, and then copy them over once you are happy with the design. Use wax pastels to outline your patterns and watercolor pencils to provide a wash of color.

CLASSIC SOPHISTICATION

Materials

- WATERCOLOR PAPER
- HB PENCIL
- ERASER
- PAINTBRUSHES
- ACRYLIC PAINTS

Always in a hurry, a busy girl with classic sophistication can nevertheless turns heads. Even when on-the-go, she always finds time to primp and carefully choose her clothes and accessories. Her appearance should be elegant, yet comfortable and versatile to accommodate a busy lifestyle!

▶ Using simple shapes, sketch the outline of the Classic Sophistication look: slim and slender. Try to give the impression of body movement.

1

2

From the first sketch, draw the complete outline of the body, as well as the details of the face, hair, and bag.

◀ Define the outfit. It should be simple, yet sophisticated: gloves, fitted jacket with high collar, black pants, and timeless, essential high heels. Complete the drawing with key accessories such as a cell phone and handbag.

YELLOW OCHRE + WHITE

GRAY

WHITE + MAGENTA + YELLOW OCHRE

VIOLET + BURNT SIENNA + WHITE

BLACK

CYAN

RED

▶ The girl with this look has very traditional taste. No need to use bold colors—black, beige, and other neutrals are perfect here. Printed jackets are very trendy and add a stylish touch. Accessories are also best in neutral tones, matching wherever possible. Classic Sophistication implies stylish perfection from head to toe!

SPORTY & ACTIVE

Sporty, active style does not have to mean a neglected look. Forget about your old jogging T-shirt; the tennis court (or wherever a favorite activity may lead) can be trendy too! Combining fashion and comfort requires an acute sense of style. Wearing a sporty and active look requires practice after practice to ensure victory—so what are you waiting for? Game, set, and match!

Materials

- WATERCOLOR PAPER
- HB PENCIL
- ERASER
- BLACK FELT-TIP MARKER
- PAINTBRUSHES
- GOUACHE PAINTS

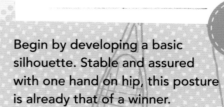

Begin by developing a basic silhouette. Stable and assured with one hand on hip, this posture is already that of a winner.

1

34

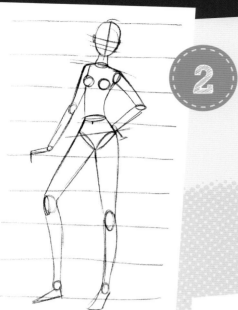

◄ Fill out the body with solid shapes, and position proportion lines over the face to place the features.

TECHNIQUE: Gouache

MAGENTA +
YELLOW OCHRE
+ WHITE

ORANGE

YELLOW

BURNT SIENNA

RED OCHRE

DARK BLUE

DARK BLUE
(DILUTED)

GRAY

BLACK

3

▶ Draw in the face, hair, and sports equipment: tennis ball in her left hand, racket in her right hand.

4

◄ Draw in the clothes. Add a shorter, pleated skirt with a spaghetti-strap tank top that stops a little short of the belly. Draw tennis shoes over the model's existing feet.

5

Outline with a black felt-tip marker, and erase unnecessary lines.

6

Mix a flesh color with a tan, and then paint exposed parts of the skin evenly. Don't forget the belly.

7

Choose a deep purple for the skirt, ribs of the shirt, and the top straps. The color of the dress is perfectly coordinated for red hair, with a few highlights. Use a light gray for the racket and a diluted yellow for the tennis ball.

8

▶ Use black paint for the shadows on the racket and white accented with purple for the hair and the folds of the skirt. Accentuate the shadows on the skin for dimension.

Complete the drawing with a few bluish shadows. The sunglasses should be large and opaque, according to trend; then draw the eyebrows. The final touch—makeup! Sporty style can be pretty and feminine even in the most extreme of situations.

Tip

TO CREATE THE EFFECT OF MOVEMENT IN THE SKIRT, PLAY WITH SHADOWS AND THE POSITION OF THE FOLDS: SLIGHTLY RAISED ON THE LEFT GIVES AN IMPRESSION OF SIZE AND MOVEMENT.

STYLISH BEACHWEAR

Finally, summer! But beware…there are no "holidays" for fashion fans. The girl wearing a Stylish Beachwear look understands this and adapts her tastes and trends to her summer wardrobe. The swimsuit is the centerpiece of her outfit, but accessories polish it up a bit.

1

Begin by sketching the basic shapes of the figure with the help of proportion lines. Don't forget to make the arm rounded in relation to where the beach ball will be.

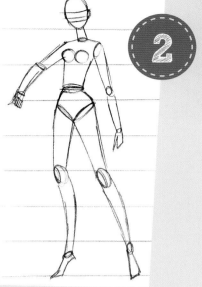

2 ◄ Outline the body contours and joints. Press firmly, as the body shape will emerge from these lines.

► Place the ball under the right arm, and draw the entire face, hair, and hat. Erase unnecessary lines.

3

4 ◄ Draw in the swimsuit, and then add accessories. Although trendy, they remain simple; beachwear should always be kept to a minimum.

5

Outline the drawing with a fine black felt-tip marker. Then draw fun patterns in the background to enhance the Stylish Beachwear look.

6

◄ With blue and red colored pencils, color in the background patterns, as well as those on the ball. Add red lips and a few strands of hair.

7

► Use blue and green for the swimsuit, pink and red for the ball, and a very opaque black (try using marker, if you like) for the hat, bag, and shoes.

The Stylish Beachwear look follows the same rule as all other fashions: No more than three dominant colors! Using black, color the flowers on the ball and the pearls in the necklace. Enhance the flowers with purple and red. Finish with polka dots on the swimsuit. A small star-shaped tattoo on the shoulder lends a playful side to the outfit. Now your model is ready to relax on the warm sand!

Tip

TO CREATE THE BACKGROUND, IT IS EASIER TO START FROM THE SILHOUETTE, BUT DO NOT MAKE IT TOO DETAILED – REMEMBER, IT SHOULD JUST BE A DECORATION!

CASUAL CHIC

The must-have piece in every casual chic look is a pair of jeans! Skirts, dresses, and high heels—generally anything too fussy—aren't necessary here. Always decked out in trousers and flats, this girl opts for comfort over an extremely girlie style. The look is still feminine, but it's all about balance!

Materials

- WATERCOLOR PAPER
- HB PENCIL
- ERASER
- BLACK FELT-TIP MARKER
- PAINTBRUSHES
- ACRYLIC PAINTS

1

Sketch a first draft of the body with proportion lines and simple shapes.

◀ Add volume to the silhouette, and add proportion lines on the face. Sketch in the hair.

▶ Erase proportion lines, and add the eyes, nose, and mouth. Sketch the clothing, including a pair of pants, belt, T-shirt, and shoulder bag.

3

RED OCHRE

WHITE +
MAGENTA +
YELLOW OCHRE

BLACK

PURPLE

GREEN

YELLOW

5

4

◀ Define the details of the shoulder bag. Then move on to define the details of the entire outfit: shirt, tank top, tote bag, scarf, cut of the pants, sneakers, buttons, and pockets. Take your time when defining the folds of clothing.

Erase unnecessary lines, and outline with a black felt-tip marker.

43

◄ Apply color evenly: red-brown for the hair, blue for the jeans, black for the shirt, and two different shades of green for the bag and scarf.

► Using the same colors in slightly lighter or darker shades, draw the folds of clothing, as well as details in the hair, shirt, and accessories.

Using a fine brush, draw in the facial features. Opt for simple makeup. Then outline some folds on the tank top and shirt, respecting the tone of each garment. Add a few small touches to create a darker contrast. Be careful not to overload your drawing with too many details: Casual Chic is a basic, effortless look!

Tip

TO KEEP THE PATTERN IN THE TANK PRECISE, YOU CAN CHOOSE TO PAINT THE STRIPES FIRST, BEFORE PAINTING THE STRAP OF THE BAG.

HOLLYWOOD GLAM

Materials

- WATERCOLOR PAPER
- HB PENCIL
- ERASER
- BLACK FELT-TIP MARKER
- PAINTBRUSHES
- ACRYLIC PAINTS

Devoted to fashion, the Hollywood Glam look is inspired by celebrities and starlets parading on the red carpet. For the girl who wears this look, it's simply out of the question to go out without being fully primped! Rain or shine, the Hollywood Glam look will sparkle—high heels, big sunglasses, and a trendy hairstyle are all key elements here. With any luck, maybe someone will mistake her for a real star!

1

To begin, choose a dynamic pose. After all, photographers and paparazzi may be nearby!

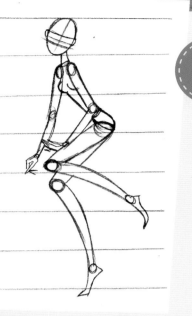

◀ Complete the silhouette by filling out the form and adding circles at the joints.

BURNT SIENNA

MAGENTA + YELLOW OCHRE + WHITE

PURPLE

YELLOW

BLACK

▶ Place the elements of the face; then draw the hair and accessories (glasses, wallet, and shoes). Erase unnecessary proportion lines and details.

3

4

◀ Define the outfit. Detail the various accessories, add the headband in her hair, and create the scarf. Then add the dress—leaving the hem short, of course!

5

Outline the drawing with a black felt-tip marker, and erase the pencil lines.

6 Choose a yellow-green and purple to color the dress. Match the headband, scarf, wallet, and shoes. Use an auburn red for the hair. The skin should appear lightly tanned.

7 Add a little black to the tights to make them opaque, and then mix with purple to match the printed dress.

8 Define a few strands of hair, and add black to the sunglasses. Add highlights on the scarf to give the effect of movement. Don't forget to add a crimson lip!

Details are essential for the Hollywood Glam look, so carefully define the prints on both the outfit and all of the accessories. Using a fine brush loaded with white, add broad edges to the dress, tights, and sunglasses for a guaranteed brilliant effect. Add light makeup, but not too heavy: This girl wants to be seen, but never look overdone!

Tip

TO TEMPER THE CONTRAST BETWEEN THE SKIN AND THE GREEN DRESS, SHADE THE ARM WITH A LITTLE BURNT SIENNA. THIS TRICK CREATES TANNED SKIN, AN ESSENTIAL FOR ANY STARLET.

RETRO CHARM

The epitome of elegance, the Retro Charm look is inspired by the resurgence of classic fashion in recent decades. This girl has adapted the vintage style to a slender silhouette. To keep things feminine, opt for plain yet timeless pieces over daring patterns and accessories. Complete the look with an attitude of graceful composure.

1

Develop the proportions of the silhouette with simple lines. This captures the characteristic pose of the Retro Charm look.

2

◀ Replace the lines with solid forms. Position proportion lines for the face, waist, and knees.

PINK
GRAY
BLACK

DARK BLUE
WHITE
BLACK
FLESH

▶ Outline the facial features and body. Erase unnecessary lines.

3

◀ Draw the clothing and accessories (including glasses, bag, belt, and shoes). Sketch in the print on the dress.

4

5

Outline the drawing with a black felt-tip marker, and erase the pencil lines.

7

Add in the details
of the outfit:
strings, buttons,
bags, etc.

6

Use gray-purple colored paper
for the background. Cut out
the white dress with scissors,
and then paste over the
background. One by one, cut
out each element of the outfit.

8

Lay in the chessboard pattern
of the dress with gray pastel,
and then complete the outfit by
adding the belt buckle and scarf.

9

Add fashionable details such as asymmetrical buttons, fringe at the bottom of the dress, and stripes on the bag. Use wax pastels for the pink cheeks. Draw in her glasses, adding a tiny layer for reflection. Be mindful to moderate the use of color and keep the clothing items and styles to a minimum—this look is modest. With a black felt-tip marker, refine the eyes, nose, mouth, and rounded chin.

Tip

EMBELLISH THE BACKGROUND TO MAKE IT DYNAMIC, AND GIVE SUBSTANCE TO THE MODEL BY ADDING SHADES OF GRAY. FORMS SHOULD BE SIMPLE FOR A HARMONIOUS EFFECT.

BOHEMIAN TRAVELER

A constant wanderer, the Bohemian Traveler is unable to remain in one place. She moves around the world, adapting her style to the various locales she visits. This look has multiple eclectic elements, including a few inspired by traditional Western and Native American styles!

1 Draw an outline of the body with a circle for the head and lines for the arms and legs. Clearly define the joints.

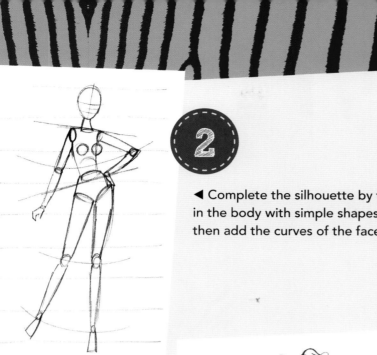

2

◄ Complete the silhouette by filling in the body with simple shapes, and then add the curves of the face.

YELLOW

PINK

PURPLE

YELLOW OCHRE

BURNT SIENNA

BLACK

► Sketch all exterior details, including the hat, hair, face, coat, and bag. Erase proportion lines, leaving the curve of the chest and a hollow at the neck.

3

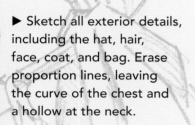

4

◄ Draw in the entire dress. This is a dress with country fringe, falling easily on the hips with a belt and tall boots. Add in jewelry.

5

Erase unnecessary lines and details, leaving only the basic design.

6

Paint the dress and coat a light yellow. Then, with a brush dipped in brown, paint the hat, belt, and boots. Use a diluted pink for the skin.

7

Slightly darken the colors, and add volume with sweeping brushstrokes that end in the shadows and folds of clothing.

8

Using red, deepen the shadows and folds of the dress. Add a shadow over the eyes and accentuate the hair with touches of purple. Paint the hat in yellow ochre, and then darken with burnt sienna and black to give it a green khaki color.

9

To suggest a background, add three diluted circles: one yellow; one purple; one red. These colors are consistent with the warm colors of the outfit, but are also reminiscent of the Wild West. Use a bit of diluted white gouache to indicate the final details, such as her headband and the capstone on her necklace.

Tip

IT'S TRICKY TO BE PRECISE WITH WATERCOLORS, ESPECIALLY IF THE COLOR IS TOO DILUTED WITH WATER BE CAREFUL NOT TO WET THE BRUSH TOO MUCH, AS IT'S DIFFICULT TO CORRECT MISTAKES!

GOTHIC

Materials

- WATERCOLOR PAPER
- HB PENCIL
- ERASER
- BLACK FELT-TIP MARKER
- WHITE, PINK, AND RED GOUACHE
- WHITE WAX PASTEL
- INDIA INK
- PAINTBRUSHES

A Gothic look swears by one color: black. This model hides her body under baggy clothes in a retro style. She is attracted to all that is morbid, such as skulls, coffins, and crosses. However, the macabre element to her style does not necessarily prevent her from being cheerful and flirtatious!

Draw an outline of the body with a circle for the head and lines for the arms and legs. Clearly define the joints.

2

◀ Refine the silhouette by adding simple shapes for the legs, arms, and neck. Place proportion lines on the face.

▶ Erase unnecessary lines, and then draw the eyes, nose, mouth, and hair. Don't forget the offset shoes.

3

4

◀ Add all of the details that pertain to the look: skirts, belts, necktie, rings, bag, and strappy shoes with stitching and prints.

5

Outline details with a black felt-tip marker, and erase unnecessary details.

59

6

Before painting with ink, consider using white wax pastel for the design of the bag, seams, etc. These small details will appear after adding the first wash of ink. Start with the lighter values; then move to the darker values. Warning: Once the ink is placed, there's no going back! Make sure your marks are intentional and precise.

Use white gouache for select details of the outfit. This technique is difficult and requires a lot of concentration!

7

Using a very fine brush, define certain details in darker black: strands of hair, straps, and belts.

8

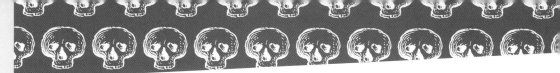

The Gothic look may involve mostly black, but you can balance it with the use of showy colors, such as red or pink. The background should remain white to highlight the silhouette, but you might consider adding colored elements on the outfit and accessories, such as knots, laces, and the bag.

Tip

INK CAN BE USED IN A MULTITUDE OF TONES, FROM VERY LIGHT TO VERY DARK, DEPENDING ON THE QUANTITY OF WATER IN THE BRUSH. TO ACHIEVE A GRADIENT, LOAD THE BRUSH WITH MORE WATER AT THE BASE OF THE BRUSH AND LESS DILUTED INK AT THE TIP. IT WILL TAKE SEVERAL TRIES TO GET IT JUST RIGHT.

BRIDAL

Materials

- DRAWING PAPER
- HB PENCIL
- ERASER
- COLORED PENCILS

The bride knows that all eyes will be on her, which means the Bridal Look must be the most beautiful in the room! This often involves a princess-like dress. Think elaborate, formal, and glamorous—the bride doesn't want to share the spotlight with anyone else!

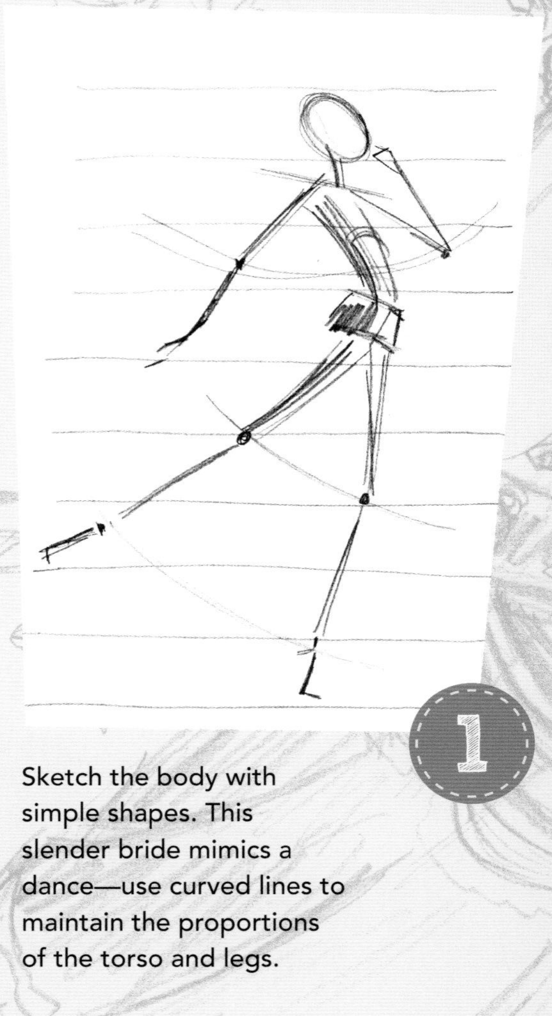

Sketch the body with simple shapes. This slender bride mimics a dance—use curved lines to maintain the proportions of the torso and legs.

2

◀ Add volume to the arms, legs, face, and neck. Sketch in the shoes—they are very high heels!

▶ Draw the hair (seen here with curls and loops in a "Marie Antoinette" style), eyes, nose, mouth, and a bouquet of flowers. Add the strapless top. Erase unnecessary pencil lines.

3

4

Draw the dress. It is substantial, composed of ruffles and drapes. Then add all the details: flowers, bows, pearls in her hair, earrings, and laced shoes.

LIGHT BLUE

BLUISH GRAY

YELLOW OCHRE

MAGENTA

DARK RED

PURPLE

GREEN

YELLOW

5

Erase unnecessary details. Keep all of the elements that will appear in the final drawing. Replace the shadows with lines indicating the folds of the dress.

6

Begin by applying light strokes of color on the hair, the corset, the top of the dress, the ruffles, and the bottom of the skirt. Apply more red roses.

7

Add a new layer of darker color, but respect the balance of the composition.

8

Use turquoise to bring out the green areas of the dress and the jewelry. Using a red colored pencil, draw wrinkles on the forearms of the gloves and emphasize the gathers of the dress.

9

The bottom of the dress must stay simple for the bride to appear stylish and sophisticated. Add a bouquet of red roses, with turquoise ribbons and birds. Using black and purple, darken the entire left side of the figure for dimension. Don't forget to give the bride light makeup in colors consistent with her outfit.

Tip

USE COLORED PENCILS TO SHADE, NOT COLOR — IT IS A DELICATE PROCESS. CAREFULLY OBSERVE A SUBJECT TO UNDERSTAND THE POSITION OF THE SHADOWS AND SHADES BEFORE YOU BEGIN.

SEASONAL LOOKS

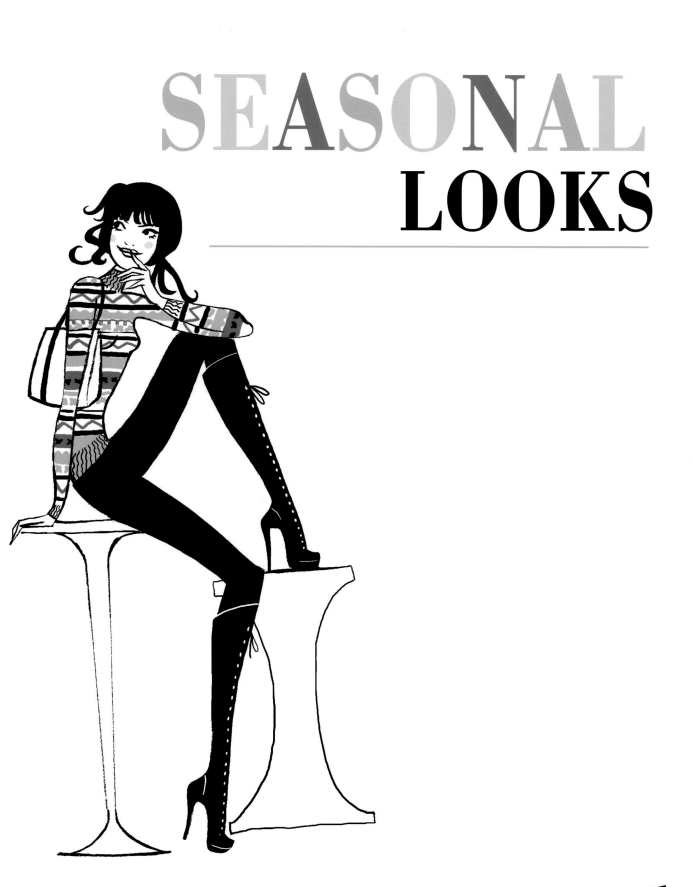

FALL SHOES

It's always difficult to leave summer behind when autumn approaches. Skirts linger in the wardrobe but must be worn with tights. Fall is the time to transition from sandals to your footwear of choice— boots, pumps, stilettos, or ballet flats.

Tights are an opportunity to create beautiful color harmonies and daring original patterns. To avoid creating a look that is too busy, shade the calf and consider adding white highlights in certain areas, depending on the material of the tights.

 With an HB pencil, sketch the legs and feet, paying particular attention to the ankle joint, represented by a circle. Then draw shoes.

 Outline the drawing in black ink with a fine brush or, for convenience, with a fine black felt-tip marker. Let dry and erase the pencil lines.

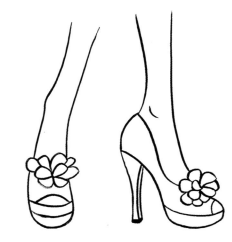

▼ Place the first layer of gouache on the areas you intend to color. Use cyan mixed with white on the body of the shoe (adding a little more white to paint the heel) and magenta mixed with white for the flower.

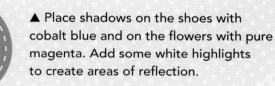

CYAN + WHITE

COBALT BLUE

MAGENTA

MAGENTA + WHITE

BLACK INK

3

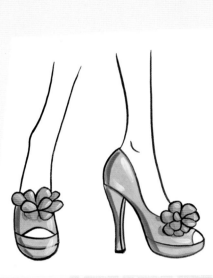

4

▲ Place shadows on the shoes with cobalt blue and on the flowers with pure magenta. Add some white highlights to create areas of reflection.

Shoe Closet

BROWN WITH A HINT OF RED AND OCHRE.

BASE OF RAW SIENNA AND BURNT UMBER; SHADE WITH PURE EARTH SIENNA.

VIOLET, WITH A LESS-DILUTED PURPLE SHADE; WHITE HIGHLIGHTS TO ADD SHINE.

WHITE WITH A TOUCH OF BURNT UMBER; BROWN BUTTONS TO CREATE THE CROCODILE PATTERN; AND WHITE ACCENTS TO HIGHLIGHT IT.

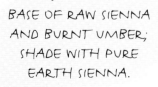

FALL BAGS

BURNT SIENNA +
A TOUCH OF WHITE

BURNT UMBER +
A TOUCH OF WHITE

BURNT SIENNA

RAW SIENNA
+ WHITE

BLACK INK

Whether a large tote to carry everything you need, a black satchel, a fancy bag with bright colors, or a clutch purse to accompany an evening dress, the range of handbag possibilities are endless in fall fashion. Just be sure to coordinate the size and color with any style you choose!

TAKE ADVANTAGE OF FOLDED ARMS TO ADD A SHORT-HANDLED BAG, CARRIED IN THE FOLD OF THE ELBOW.

1 Create simple forms with an HB pencil. For the body of the bag, start by drawing rectangles with rounded corners.

2 Using a fine brush, outline the drawing in ink, let dry, and erase the pencil lines.

With a thicker brush, apply black ink on the handles and body of the bag.

For the leather and stitching, add a layer of raw sienna mixed with white, and then mark the shadows with pure raw sienna. For the grid pattern, start by adding horizontal bands in burnt umber mixed with a touch of white. Next draw the darker vertical stripes in burnt umber. Finish with very diluted touches of burnt umber on the metal rings and a bit of white gouache to highlight the handles.

Fingerless Gloves

Thanks to the fingers being cut off, fingerless gloves are more functional than full gloves. They are also less warm, making them ideal for mid-season fashion. They can be made out of leather, plain and simple wool, or patterned material. Practice drawing hands in all positions before you accessorize (see page 82).

Bag Collection

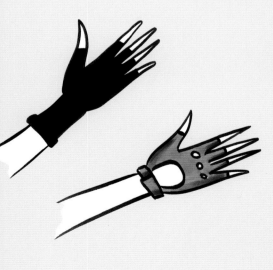

71

FALL HATS & SCARVES

Pairing a felt hat with a beautiful shawl or scarf is the latest chic trend! But don't forget to style the hair and accessorize with a pair of glasses. To dress things down—and add extra style to the outfit—add a jacket with a wide neck.

▶ Sketch the hat with an HB pencil. Start from the head, and deepen the hat: first the edges, and then the top. Don't forget to place the band around the center.

A SIMPLE HAT GIVES A SOPHISTICATED TOUCH TO ANY LOOK, AS LONG AS IT COORDINATES WITH THE JACKET.

◀ Outline the drawing with ink, and place two lines on top of the hat to indicate volume. Erase the pencil lines.

▶ Fill in the body of the hat with black ink. For the band, use gouache: a mixture of burnt sienna, ochre, and white. Add touches of dark brown to shade. Finish by adding a few touches of white all over.

Hairstyles & Accessories

BURNT SIENNA

BURNT SIENNA
+ OCHRE
+ WHITE

BLACK INK

A COLLAR SHOULD CHANGE AND
ADJUST SHAPE DEPENDING ON
WHETHER THE JACKET IS OPEN
OR CLOSED—IT CAN CHANGE THE
ENTIRE ATTITUDE OF THE OUTFIT!

Tip

CREATE LEOPARD PRINT BY APPLYING BEIGE ON THE
BOTTOM. THEN ADD SPOTS: ADD SMALL TOUCHES OF
BLACK (INK OR ACRYLIC) WITH AN ALMOST-DRY BRUSH
LIGHTLY-LOADED WITH COLOR, AND THEN FINISH WITH A
TOUCH OF BROWN WITHIN EACH PATTERN.

73

FALL LOOK

A classic style can be easily accessorized with touches of whimsy: carefully selected jewelry, a printed sweater, and a fringed skirt. The right shoes bring charm and originality to the overall look—a perfect snapshot of the season's character, adapted to all situations at all times!

▼ Sketch a simplified model, and add dimension by rounding the joints and angling the hips in line with the shoulders and spine.

1

Tip

MAKE SMALL SKETCHES IN FELT-TIP MARKER TO FIND THE PERFECT COLOR RANGE BEFORE YOU BEGIN.

②

▶ Add volume to the silhouette. Draw proportion lines over the face to place the nose, eyes, and mouth.

Tip

·····

TAKE ADVANTAGE OF THIS STEP BY WIDENING THE LEGS SLIGHTLY; THIS WILL GIVE YOUR MODEL BETTER SUPPORT TO REST A HAND ON HER HIP.

③

◀ Work in details and sketch the dress, erasing unnecessary lines that clutter the design. Add accessories, such as the jewelry, shoes, hat, umbrella, and bag.

④

▶ Outline the drawing with a fine black felt-tip marker. Erase the pencil lines. Add one or two leaves in the background to bring context to your drawing.

75

◀ Using tracing paper, trace the drawing from step 4 in pencil, and then redraw the outline in black as before. Begin adding the lightest colors, starting with the skin.

▶ Continue to add in color: very diluted purple for the shirt, a sienna mixture for the jacket and hat-band, a mixture of diluted cyan and white for the shoes, strong orange for the hair, and bright red for the tights.

◀ Use pure black for the skirt. Shade the drawing using the same tones, but more diluted. For the print and shadows on the tights, add a touch of black to the red. The print on the blouse can be accentuated with pure purple. For the bag and hat, refer back to pages 70–73. Don't forget to add details!

Jewelry

Use bracelets to create different styles. Add subtle hints of color, such as a red ring with matching tights. To enhance the image, leave some details without color—jewelry lends itself well to this delicate color treatment.

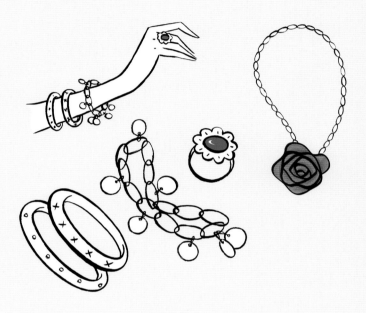

Makeup

Use warm colors for natural makeup shades: pink, red, and brown. To enhance the complexion of the model without being too flashy, add a touch of mascara. The eyes are deep blue, perfectly matched to the shirt!

8

Highlight contrasts with tiny buttons. Add makeup. Finally, correct any small errors with a little diluted white gouache, if necessary.

WINTER HANDBAGS

TECHNIQUE: Gouache

CYAN + WHITE

CYAN

OCHRE + WHITE

BURNT SIENNA

OCHRE

Fur is a necessity to protect oneself from the harsh temperatures of winter. You'll even find it on handbags! Try playing up the effects of the material, and create interesting contrasts between smooth and shiny leather and full fur or fluffy wool. Remember that adding cheerful colors to brighten your piece can create a strong impact for even the most subtle of outfits.

1 Sketch the bag using simple shapes, and then erase the corners.

2 Outline the sketch with a black felt-tip marker. Trace the ripples of fur along the pockets, and add small strokes around the pompoms. Erase any unnecessary lines.

3 Apply colors: a mixture of cyan, white, and a touch of yellow ochre for the fabric of the bag; use the same mixture with much less white for the handles.

Shade the bag with a darker blue. Add a little black to the mixture for the shadows on the handles. For fur, paint a beige background made of yellow ochre, white, and a touch of burnt sienna. Then add touches of the same mixture, but darker. Color the metal rings with yellow ochre. Finish with some white highlights on the metal rings to give them shine.

Bag Collection

WINTER BOOTS & HATS

From head to toe, nothing is left exposed in winter! Make your winter look snow-ready with boots and a fur hat. For a more glamorous city style, we'll use leather waders, but beware of slipping!

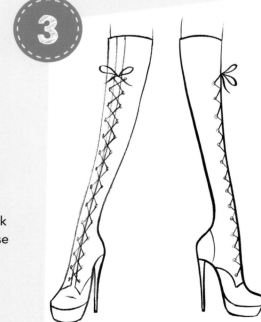

1

◄ Outline the ankles and feet for proportion.

2

◄ Draw boots on the feet, making sure that the heel is straight. Create a wedge heel in the front, and take care to follow the line of the shin when placing the laces.

3

► Outline the drawing with a black felt-tip marker. Erase the pencil lines.

Paint the boots with a mixture of purple and white gouache.

Shade with pure purple, and add some white highlights for reflection on the polished leather. Use a felt-tip marker to outline any details that were covered with gouache.

Winter Hats & Collars

There's nothing like a big fur collar to feel warm in winter! Fur brings a nice chic touch to any winter look.

WINTER GLOVES & BELTS

The primary purpose of gloves is to keep the hands warm, but they are also a true fashion accessory. Between fine leather gloves, long gloves in multicolored wool, or even mittens, you have plenty of choices! To keep your much needed layers in place, a belt is also a wardrobe staple.

Hands Study

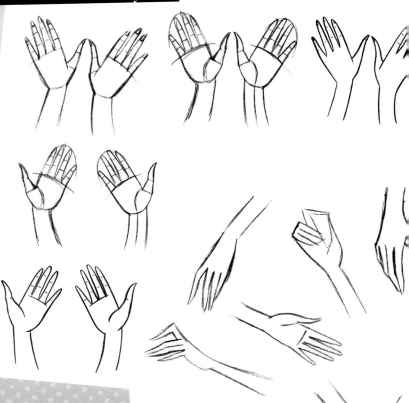

To render gloves or simply accentuate the realism of models, we must consider the shape of the hands and the way they are drawn. Study the similarities and differences between the backs and palms, as well as the arrangement of the fingers in different positions.

Gloves

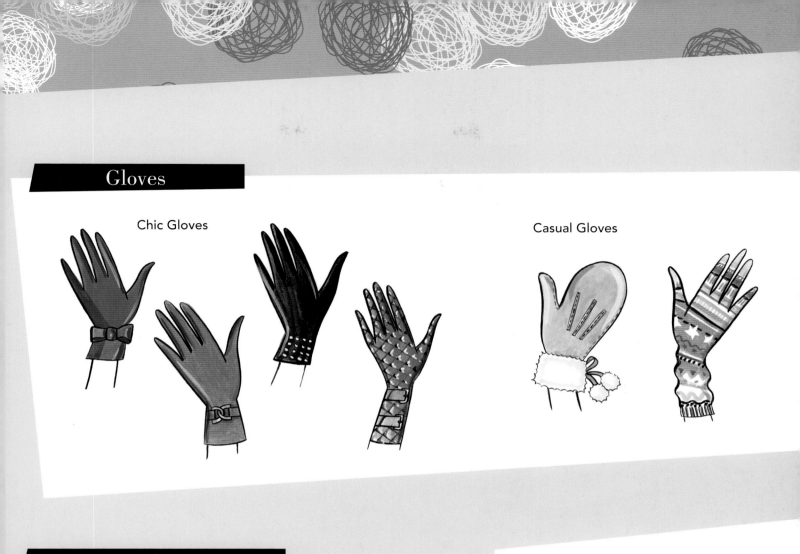

Chic Gloves

Casual Gloves

Belts

The belt is traditionally found on pant loops, but you can also add one as a purely decorative accessory over pants or a tunic. Choose a contrasting color, or create a monochromatic blend. Flexible belts also add a casual effect. Remember, whether necessary or decorative, open or tied closed, a belt always affects the way the fabric falls.

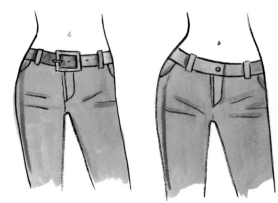

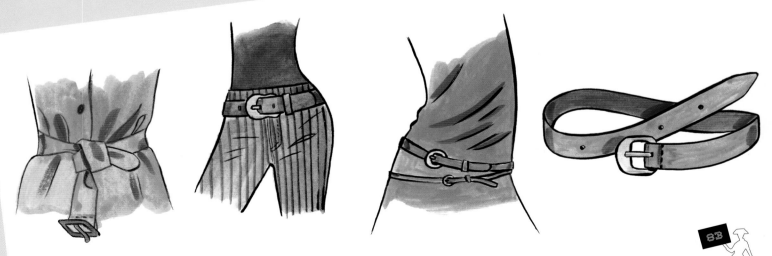

WINTER LOOK

To be fashionable in all circumstances, there is nothing like the perfect pair of high boots in black leather, worn with a stylish fur-lined coat. The simple, cool colors of this outfit can be enhanced with a few well-chosen accessories in a contrasting color such as yellow.

Construct the silhouette with simple shapes, being mindful of proportions. The body is partially folded, so the figure is a little smaller, but the chest and legs remain unchanged. The joints on the body should be symmetrical—they give the silhouette credibility.

1

2

Refine the silhouette while staying proportionate. Draw a line of symmetry on the face, neck, and chest; add volume to the arms and legs; and make a draft sketch of the fingers.

3

▶ Work in details and dress your model. Don't forget the accessories: bags, jewelry, boots, and a fur-trimmed coat.

YELLOW OCHRE

MAGENTA + YELLOW OCHRE + WHITE

PURPLE + WHITE

GRAY

BLACK

YELLOW

DARK PINK

COBALT BLUE

RED

4

◀ Outline the drawing with a black felt-tip marker, and erase the last pencil lines.

5

▶ Trace the drawing from step 4, but don't pay much attention to the details. Begin coloring the areas of skin.

85

6 Add a layer of purple mixed with white on the coat.

7 Use black on the hair, gloves, and boots, and a very light gray on the ends of the fur coat. Shade the coat, fur, and skin with the same colors, but in darker tones. Draw facial details. Use pure white for the eyes and mouth.

With a darker gray, detail the fur. Put some white highlights with a hint of purple on the boots, gloves, and hair. Don't forget the last details, including the bag, bracelet, coat pocket, and makeup.

Jewelry

Fine jewelry and delicate charms create a bit of contrast with the thick and fluffy materials often found in winter clothes. Choose a dress with a single well-defined color, which contrasts sharply with the rest of the outfit, or use jewelry to create a colorful reminder of these elements.

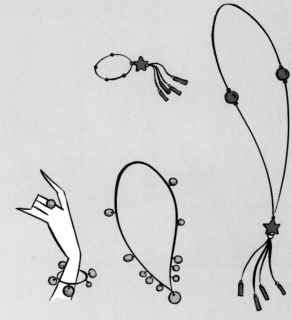

Makeup

For a sophisticated look, it's important to choose colors that match the outfit. Here, pink, red, and purple colors contrast with the blue eyes and are reminiscent of the coat. This gives an impression of elegance and sobriety.

SPRING SHOES

Spring looks imply the start of a lighter, more effortless style, including shoes! Whether you choose gladiator sandals or flip flops, include careful, delicate details like straps or ribbons to equip you for all the fresh activity that comes along with spring!

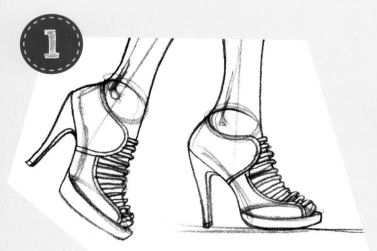

KNOTTED STRAPS, FLOWERS, POLKA DOTS, NEUTRAL OR COLORED, WITH OR WITHOUT SOCKS...IT'S UP TO THE IMAGINATION!

1

▲ With an HB pencil, sketch the feet, keeping the ankle and leg position in mind. Form the shoe around the shape of the foot.

2

▶ Outline the drawing with a black felt-tip marker. Erase the pencil lines.

3

Apply a layer of red gouache to the shoes. Add a mixture of red with more or less yellow on the edges of the shoe and heel.

4

Shade the shoes with burnt sienna, and then add white highlights for shine.

Shoe Closet

SPRING BAGS & HATS

Full of polka dots, flowers, and soft colors, spring is a season packed with personality. Use your imagination to create the outfit that best suits your needs, integrating all the necessary accessories, such as bags and hats.

▶ Sketch the bag in pencil. The shape is an elongated rectangle. Then draw the handles, polka dots, and folds of fabric. Outline the drawing with a black felt-tip marker.

TECHNIQUE: Acrylic

YELLOW + GREEN

PINK

YELLOW

PURPLE + WHITE

BLACK

RED

◀ Paint the polka dots in various colors.

◀ Paint the handles and the edges of the bag with yellow, adding a touch of green. Shade the bag with a very diluted blue and with a fairly diluted green for the handles.

GREEN YELLOW OCHRE

DARK
ORANGE ORANGE

With a pencil, sketch the head of the young woman and build the hat around it. Add all the details.

Outline the drawing with a black felt-tip marker. Add black on the lips, hair, and the shadow of the neck.

Apply a first layer of gouache.

Shade your drawing with the same colors, and paint in the green floral motifs.

Hatbox

Be creative and have fun with extravagant hat finishes.

SPRING SCARVES & BELTS

Whether for sun protection, to tame flyaways, or just to bring an extra touch of color, the scarf fits into all types of personal style. Longer scarves can also be used as a belt, tied at the waist or hips.

Scarves

Useful and elegant, a light fabric protects against the spring breeze. To make the material fluid and transparent, use a very diluted paint to allow the drawing to show through.

A beautiful polka-dotted scarf knotted (the way Grace Kelly would have worn it!) with a pair of sixties-style sunglasses remains timeless!

A pretty folded scarf can easily be used as a headband.

Colorful printed scarves rolled and tied around a high bun give a guaranteed bohemian effect!

Lightly tie the scarf around the neck for a youthful look.

Belts

Accessorized with a big bow at the waist, some jewelry, big sunglasses, and an original hairstyle, a simple black dress is a winner every time.

One scarf to emphasize the waist, and another to accessorize a handbag—the scarf is an accessory that customizes even the most classic outfits.

A broad scarf knotted loosely on the hips accentuates the movement of a full skirt.

SPRING LOOK

Dynamic and buzzing with activity, the Spring Look must have an elegant and comfortable fit. A skirt with pockets matched with a simple T-shirt proves this look is all about convenience. Bright colors and a few well-chosen accessories bring originality and sophistication to the set.

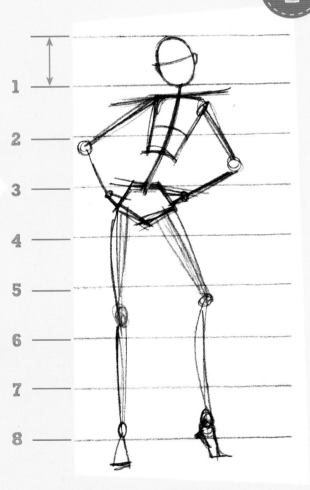

1

Outline the silhouette with simple shapes. Add proportion lines, forming joints in line with the shoulders and hips.

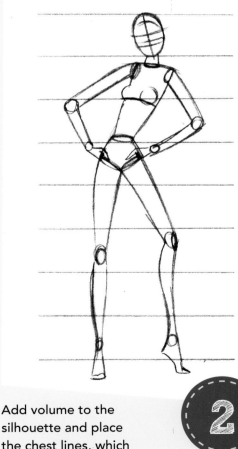

2

Add volume to the silhouette and place the chest lines, which should be in line with the facial features.

3

Add the details step by step. First add the clothing, then the footwear, and then the many accessories, such as the bag, jewelry, sunglasses, and scarf. Don't forget the makeup!

FLESH

ORANGE

PINK

YELLOW

RED

CYAN

BROWN

DARK BROWN

4

Outline the drawing with a black felt-tip marker, and erase the pencil lines.

5

Trace the drawing from step 4 without paying too much attention to detail. Start applying color in solids.

6

Next shade your drawing with colors that are a little more shaded (add red in the skin color, etc.). Use a mixture of blue and white in the shadows of the bag. Start adding some details, including facial features and bracelets.

7 Add a second shadow layer for more support. Finalize the details, including the printed polka-dot skirt, necklace, belt details, red high heels, reflections in the glasses, and makeup.

Jewelry

Discrete accessories and pretty jewelry are best here—a plain and simple chain complete with round buttons brings a touch of color. You can also add a few charms for fun!

Makeup

When creating makeup for a fresh season, settle for less: subtle green eyelids, pink lips, and a touch of blush on the cheekbones—plus mascara to get the eyes fluttering!

SUMMER HATS

GREEN

YELLOW + CYAN

PINK

Summer is the season for weddings and outdoor festivities, making it the perfect opportunity to wear beautiful hats! Wide-brimmed options should be carefully coordinated with the outfit. But don't forget the hair—the hat can't stay on forever!

First build the head, and then the hat. Draw a large, horizontal brim with ellipsed edges and a semi-circle overlooking the head. Add details such as the ribbon, bow, and face.

Outline the drawing with a black felt-tip marker. Erase all pencil lines. Apply black on the hair and under the chin to form the shadow.

Paint a grid of horizontal and vertical lines across the hat with a mixture of yellow and cyan. Color the bow with the same mixture. Add green shadows. Finish with facial details, including blue eyes and pink lips and cheeks.

Hairstyles

Choose the hairstyle based on your desired effect and style: short cut for a boyish look, adorned with a colorful flower, wavy and loose, or slicked over to one side. For light hair colors, add reflections in certain places to animate the hair.

Hatbox

Whether you choose a chic tomboy hat, a cowboy hat, or a pink hat with a wide rim, it's essential to stay protected from the sun.

SUMMER SHOES & BAGS

Summer shoes should be elegant, comfortable, and bold—but always in harmony with the rest of the outfit. A small handbag is best, to save space as well as be light and portable for all of those spur-of-the-moment summer activities!

Shoe Closet

Summer is the season of choice for open-toed shoes: sandals, gladiator sandals, and slip-ons. It also offers the largest array of colors and materials (flip flops, colored plastic, wood, cork, fabric, etc.). Finally, because the feet are exposed, feel free to add ornaments, big bows, beads, charms, or even ribbons to tie around the ankle.

TECHNIQUE: Gouache

MAGENTA +
WHITE

YELLOW +
WHITE +
YELLOW OCHRE

1

Use a rectangle to visualize the bag's proportions, but soften the edges by rounding all angles and slightly collapsing the middle. Then add the details and creases.

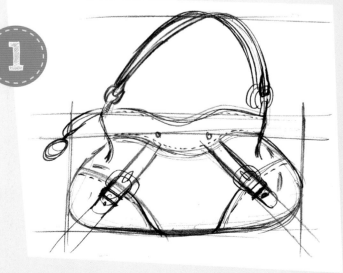

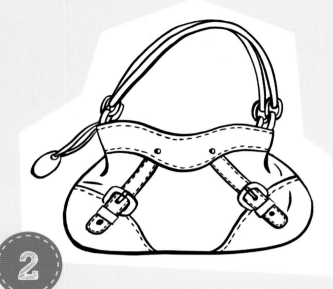

2

Outline the drawing with a black felt-tip marker, ensuring a variety of line thicknesses. Erase unnecessary pencil lines.

3

Paint the leather edges and handles with a mixture of magenta and white gouache. With this same mixture, draw smooth horizontal lines on the fabric portion of the bag.

4

Draw vertical lines to complete the gingham pattern. Shade everything with magenta to give a little more dimension. For the metal clasps, use a mixture of yellow, yellow ochre, and white. Add a very thin black line around select areas to keep the paint vibrant.

Bag Collection

A PINK BAG FOR A HIP NIGHT OUT; A METALLIC BLUE BAG FOR A CLASSY EVENING; AND AN ORANGE BAG WITH A GOLDEN CLASP TO COMPLEMENT A DARK-COLORED DRESS.

SUMMER LIGHT ACCESSORIES & OUTFITS

To be the most beautiful beachgoer, everything is taken into consideration, down to the smallest accessory. In a light swimsuit or coordinated bikini dress, the model wearing this look shelters herself nonchalantly behind sunglasses and a fan.

Fans

Whether ornately patterned or classic lace, the range of fabrics found in fans evokes the feeling of irresistibly hot summer nights. The style of fan can utterly transform the look too—the combination of blue with pink gingham makes the mood feel feminine and delicate.

Tip

KEEP A HINT OF TRANSPARENCY IN THE FRAME, SO THAT THE DESIGN REMAINS VISIBLE.

Glasses

How to wear glasses is also important: Worn as a headband, they are more than a fashion accessory, and worn on the nose, they invite mischievous glances.

Tip

SUNGLASSES HAVE MULTIPLE REFLECTIONS: PLACE A LARGE DARK AREA FIRST, AND THEN ADD COLOR KEYS A LITTLE LIGHTER THAN THE BASE.

Chic, glamorous, or sporty, sunglasses give an immediate indication of style. Are you framed to see life in pink, dreamy blue, or aviator?

Swimwear

With this little blue dress, accessories should be simple to avoid overwhelming the outfit but still unify the colors in the dress. To vary the items the model holds, replace the dress with a sarong skirt and bikini top.

Striped, solid, or polka dot, bikinis are the center of summer fashion. Play with materials: Stripes placed next to each other without a clearly marked outline give a stitched effect, while combining the top with a high-waist boxer produces a sweet retro charm.

Tip

FOR SHADING, CONTRAST WITH TOUCHES OF BRIGHT COLOR, USING A NEUTRAL COLOR (VERY DARK BROWN) TO DILUTE. DIFFERENT BASE COLORS WILL STILL BE VISIBLE, MAKING THE DRAWING MORE REALISTIC.

SUMMER SWIMWEAR

No need for a ton of accessories to be elegant on the beach. The style statement is made simply with the choice of swimsuit. Choose a bikini with or without straps to suit a more or less active day, but always opt for one that will best enhance the silhouette.

With pure color and a nice fabric, it's the simple details that make a difference: a small fringe under the bra, pretty matching shoes, and voilà!

It's not always easy to wear white, but it has some advantages—it brings out a good tan and also allows you to choose bright accessories.

For sunbathing without tan lines, opt for a strapless bikini with a low-waisted bottom tied on the sides. Avoid overloading on accessories: a pair of glasses will suffice.

The most essential and
practical accessory for a
summer look, a beach bag
can be chosen in a pattern
or color coordinated
with the bikini.

For those who do not want to show their legs,
or simply wish to be a little more formal, try a
sarong or large towel tied around the waist.
Walking on the beach on high heels armed
with a towel and basket is a perilous exercise,
but one that is sure to get you noticed!

The minimalist black bikini always
creates a beautiful effect, with
just a small knot on the side to
add definition to the look.

SUMMER LOOK

Summer is often about travel, and the vacationer wants to be comfortable enough to carry the essentials she needs for the trip, including a suitcase and, sometimes, even a pet! Accessories in the Summer Look definitely need to be practical—such as a simple hairband to keep the hair out of the eyes and the sunglasses from slipping. But just because the weather warms up doesn't mean style has to be abandoned— the blend of pink and blue in a coordinating gingham print are perfectly chic!

▶ Sketch the silhouette with simple shapes. Pay special attention to the folded arm at the bust. Draw lightly behind the bust so that you can see how it connects to the shoulder.

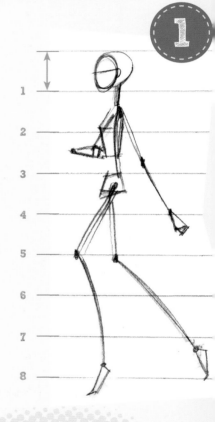

1

2

◀ Add a little volume to the silhouette, and place the proportion lines of the face. Carefully draw the hands, the little dog in her arms, and her ponytail.

3

Detail the shirt and dress. Add the accessories—handbag, headband, sunglasses, jewelry, shoes, and of course the little dog! Finally, add the gingham patterns to the skirt and headband. Erase pencil lines as you go.

FLESH

MAGENTA + WHITE

CYAN + WHITE

GREEN

BROWN

YELLOW + YELLOW OCHRE

YELLOW OCHRE

VIOLET

BLACK

Outline the drawing with a black felt-tip marker. Continue to add some finer details, such as the label on the bag, the gloves, and one last shopping bag. Erase the last pencil lines.

4

5 Start coloring the skin and hair. For the hair, first apply a coat of yellow mixed with a little yellow ochre, and then paint a few strands with pure yellow ochre.

On the skirt, trace a fairly tight grid for the gingham with cyan gouache, adding a little white. For the bag and shoes, use a mixture of magenta and pink (see page 101 for the handbag).

6

7

Apply a coat of black gouache on the tank top, the headband, and the dog's collar. Place some shadows with darker or contrasting colors (very diluted pink on the skirt and scarf, and a very diluted blue on the suitcase and shoes). Shade the dog with yellow ochre.

Jewelry

Combine chains with small pendants of various shapes in beautiful, bright colors—a blue butterfly, a gingham heart, cherries, or an ice cream cone—anything goes! Opt for delicate colored bracelets to add a touch of charm without overwhelming the look.

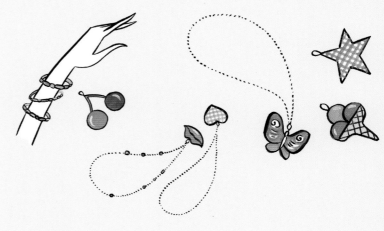

Makeup

Makeup for a fresh, seasonal look includes a relatively discreet blue eye shadow (created with a diluted mixture of cyan and white), which contrasts nicely with bright red-pink lips (pure magenta). Emphasize the cheekbones with a touch of pink blush (mixture of magenta and white) for a more dapper look.

fashion DESIGNER
LOOKS

THE SKETCHBOOK

The secret of every designer? Observation! Seek inspiration from the people around you for your sketches. Use real life examples to help you understand the proportions of the human body. When you come to your drawing paper, the most important thing is to render solid proportions and try to represent the personality of the model in your drawing. This allows you to be more comfortable styling the silhouette and bring a personal touch to your finished piece.

TECHNIQUE:
Thick Felt-tip Marker

Work the outline quickly with a single tool to start (I used a thick felt-tip marker.) Try to understand the nature of the silhouette: Is it slender, boyish, or curvy? The attitude of the model is also crucial. Decide now what your pose will be: nonchalant, arched, or relaxed.

PARIS, OCTOBER

NEW YORK, NOVEMBER 17

LONG BELTED COAT, TAPERED LEGS, AND POINTY BOOTS CHARACTERIZE THIS SILHOUETTE. BE SURE TO ADD MOVEMENT IN THE HAIR TO MAKE THE SKETCH COME TO LIFE.

HAT, LONG SCARF, FLARED COAT, AND HIGH BOOTS: THIS FIGURE IS HEAD-TO-TOE BOHEMIAN.

MEGÈVE, FEBRUARY 8

TRY TO KEEP THINGS
CLEAN IN WINTER, AND
SKETCH SILHOUETTES
WRAPPED UP IN THEIR
SWEATERS. HATS, COZY
SCARVES, AND COATS ARE
A MUST!

BERLIN, JUNE 10

CASUAL, FORWARD-FACING
SILHOUETTES EMPHASIZE
THE FOLDS OF JEANS AND
SWEATERS. NONCHALANT
SILHOUETTES MIGHT
INCLUDE A HAND IN THE
POCKET, A DREAMY LOOK,
AND A RELAXED POSE.

LONDON, MAY 20

DRAW THE OUTLINE OF THE
SILHOUETTE IN A PROFILE
VIEW. DON'T FOCUS ON
EXPRESSIONS OR OTHER
DETAILS. THE THICK LINES
ARE IMPACTFUL AND
SUGGEST A STUDIOUS STYLE
FOR THE MODEL.

FINE-LINE MARKER

The felt tip of a fine-line marker allows for detailing facial features, as well as the style of the dress. For a chic and sophisticated element, add a handbag or a pair of high-heeled shoes.

USE A FINE-TIP MARKER TO SHADE A LEG AND DETAIL PARTS OF THE OUTFIT.

TECHNIQUE:
Fine-line Marker

ALICE, A FOLLOWER OF RETAIL FASHION

VALENTINE FAN HANDBAGS

DOE EYES, ÉPAULETTES, AND A KNOTTED BELT ARE THE KEY STRENGTHS OF THIS OUTFIT.

BALLPOINT PEN & GRAPHITE PENCIL

Unlike thick felt marker, ballpoint pen layers extremely well. Alternate strong and fine lines to mark the folds of clothing, and then shade certain parts to create contrast.

TECHNIQUE:
Ballpoint Pen

WITH THE BALLPOINT PEN, THE GOAL IS NOT TO MAKE A PERFECT LINE THE FIRST TIME: GO OVER THE SAME LINE SEVERAL TIMES AND TAKE THE OPPORTUNITY TO CHANGE THINGS AS THE SKETCH IS FORMED.

FOCUS ON THE PROPORTIONS OF THE BODY AND NOT ON THE DETAILS. LAYERING THE OUTLINE GIVES YOU ROOM TO EXPERIMENT.

TECHNIQUE:
Graphite Pencil

Pencil allows for shading in the clothing—blur some details and emphasize others.

ALTHOUGH THE MAIN ADVANTAGE OF PENCIL IS THAT IT ERASES EASILY, CHALLENGE YOURSELF TO ERASE AS LITTLE AS POSSIBLE TO IMPROVE YOUR SKILLS!

115

INK & COLORED PENCIL

Get inspired by your own wardrobe—look into your closet and see what can be used to create unique outfits for your drawing. If you're working with colors and shapes that you love and flipping through favorite fashion magazines, your models will be one-of-a-kind and perfectly on trend!

YELLOW

YELLOW OCHRE

ORANGE

BLUE

BLACK INK

1 Plan a quick sketch before beginning work on your final support. Large-format drawing or marker paper is my support of choice.

2 Outline the drawing with a black felt-tip marker, moving in rapid and spontaneous gestures, and then erase the pencil lines. Use colored pencils for the stripes (yellow, yellow ochre, orange, and blue) and a brush dipped in ink for the neckline and skirt. Choose blue and green eyeshadow and pink for the mouth. For the cheeks, blend with a pink pencil.

BLACK

BLUE

PURPLE

RED

FLESH

WHITE

PENCIL & MARKER

Begin with a pencil sketch on your paper. Use quick strokes, and don't worry about details.

2

Trace the outline of the silhouette with a fine felt-tip marker, except for the legs. At this point, it is easy to change details, such as the position of the head, hands, and feet. Fill in the coat with thick black marker, and add highlights with white. Feel free to create light effects or gradients, working in the white ink with your finger before it dries. Use blue for the jeans and add contrast with touches of purple. Use a skin color for the cheeks and a touch of red for the lips. Erase the pencil lines in some places, or keep them to bring relief to the drawing.

WATERCOLOR & PASTEL

TECHNIQUE: Mixed Media
(Watercolor & Wax Pastel)

BLACK

YELLOW

FLESH

RED

BLUE

1

Make a pencil sketch from a magazine photo. Then trace the sketch onto grained paper. It's best to draw several versions of the sketch so that you can change the details at your convenience.

2 ▶ Apply a white wax pastel to the figure's sleeves and jacket. With a yellow wax pastel, draw the bag. Then move to watercolor, starting with the lighter tones: flesh, red, and then black. Outline some details in black pencil to fill out the sketch, including the sleeves, a belt, and shoes.

Variation

FOR A SLIGHTLY DIFFERENT STYLE, USE WHITE PASTEL TO DRAW SPIRAL SHAPES ON THE SLEEVES AND YELLOW PASTEL TO ADD VERTICAL LINES ON THE JACKET. CRISSCROSS THE BAG WITH BLUE PASTEL. THEN PAINT WITH WATERCOLOR. ENHANCE SOME DETAILS WITH BLACK PENCIL, AND FINISH BY ADDING A BELT IN BLUE PASTEL.

HAUTE COUTURE

The greatest designers design haute couture collections twice a year as emblems of their brand and trademark style. The choice of fabrics and cut of the garments are crucial—haute couture is known for eccentric outfits, which can hardly be worn in everyday life, but bring new energy to fashion and inspire future trends.

1

Begin with a sketch for research. Limit the number of details and the volume of the clothes.

2

Trace lightly with a black pencil. Draw only the main outlines, without the sleeves, to maximize the transparency effect.

Tip

WORK ON PAPER THAT IS AT LEAST 9.5" X 12.5" TO ACCOMMODATE FOR BROAD OUTLINES AND RELEASE GESTURES. THEN MIMIC THE COLOR SCHEME BY CHOOSING UP TO FOUR COLORS, ACCORDING TO YOUR DESIRED LOOK. USE TOOLS ADAPTED TO THE FORMAT, SUCH AS A BROAD BRUSH, LARGE BRUSH, AND A CRAYON. SUGGEST KEY FEATURES FOR THE EYE TO FOCUS ON, AND LEAVE THE REST TO THE IMAGINATION.

RED + BLACK

YELLOW OCHRE + PURPLE

To create patterns, pleats, and highlights, apply a touch of paint and scrape with the tip of the brush handle. To render sheer fabric, apply flesh color first and let dry. Then dilute acrylic (I used purple) with plenty of water to create a wash, and apply over the skin tone. The colors don't need to be precise. You can mix several shades of red, with a little purple or yellow ochre. Use a brush to paint the drapes of fabric. Working with your fingers, create material and shading (for the thigh and some drapes of fabric).

YOUR COLLECTION

It's time to start creating your own collection. The important thing is to gather ideas and find a theme: gingham, fairy tales, film, 1960s, European... Define the spirit of your collection with patterns or costumes that inspire you. To tie everything together and give unity to your pieces, don't use more than six colors, and draw all of the silhouettes in the same pose.

1 Begin by making a pencil sketch of different clothes and accessories that match your selected style. Determine your trends; here a simple, flouncy skirt becomes the main element of the outfit. Polka dots or stripes give it even more charm! A slightly ruffled shirt is the perfect complement. Choose pieces that stand out, and experiment with original or unexpected touches. Sunglasses in a heart shape provide a playful look. The final touch? Add a bandana, the ideal summer accessory!

BLACK

CYAN

2

Trace your pencil sketch onto drawing paper using a black pencil. Use a felt-tip marker to color the clothes and a black felt brush for the eyes and other details. For polka dots and other details, use a white paint marker.

◄ An outfit cannot be complete without a purse! On the shoulder, bucket-style, or with handles and polka dots—it's best to be selective to cultivate a collection worthy of your own name! The blue lagoon shade provides the dominant color here. Imagine what is likely to appeal to your audience. Ideally, you want to be inspired by magazines, but also create according to the consumer's taste. It's a balancing act!

BLACK

CYAN

RED

1 A full skirt instantly creates a feminine, doll-like look. Feel free to experiment with fun, flashy accessories, such as a pair of statement earrings, a bow at the waist, or a small bag in the crook of the elbow. Create a look unique to your own style and vision!

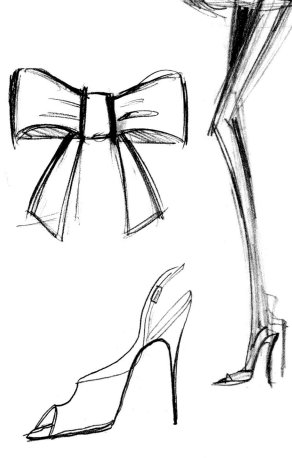

An icon of the 1960s, the blue gingham print is timeless. This pattern is created by crossing two blue felt-tip marker strokes over one another. To enhance the effect, add slightly darker points where the lines cross.

PERFECTLY PAIRED WITH A
LITTLE BLACK CAP, THIS DRESS
HAS CHARM. PLAY WITH
DIFFERENT OPTIONS AND
CHOOSE ANY STYLE OF HAT.

PURPLE

GREEN

CYAN

BLACK

This look has a "hippie chic" vibe with a tunic, rolled jeans, linen trousers, and a scarf—an outfit perfect for summer! From your own wardrobe, try to compose an outfit that will give a nod to trends of the past, while remaining relevant to current fashions. To do this, add polka dots to the tunic and differentiate the type of jewelry (I used plastic here). The choice of handbag is also key, because it must fit perfectly with the developed style.

1

2

CHOOSE BRIGHT COLORS THAT
COMPLEMENT ONE ANOTHER
AGAINST A CONTRASTING
BACKGROUND.

Tip

HAVE FUN BY ADDING VARIETY TO YOUR OUTFIT. ADD RUFFLES, BUTTONS, OR EVEN CHANGE THE SHAPE OF THE NECKLINE. WITH MORE VARIATIONS, THE COLLECTION WILL ONLY GET BETTER — SELECT COMPLEMENTARY COLORS AND USE YOUR IMAGINATION!

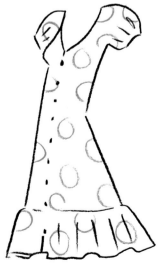
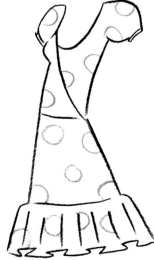

I grew up in Lyon, France, where a love for drawing naturally led me to the La Martinière Terreaux School of Applied Arts, where my passion for artistic anatomy and live models was born. After arriving in Paris to join the school of Art Olivier de Serres, I quickly turned to fashion design. What source of inspiration could be better than Paris? For the past 20 years, I've done freelance advertising and publishing work for women's magazines. In *Fashion Design Lookbook*, you will find essential tips and technical advice on how to create original sketches and even your own ready-to-wear collection! Once you've acquired the techniques, keep in mind that a unique eye and the ability to be spontaneous are true assets to defining your own style. Finally, keep in mind that a sketch cannot be successful without enthusiasm, so enjoy the process! I hope you have as much fun learning to draw from these models as I did creating them!

Blandine Lelarge